"Let's go up on the hill," said Sam to Kim and Ravi.

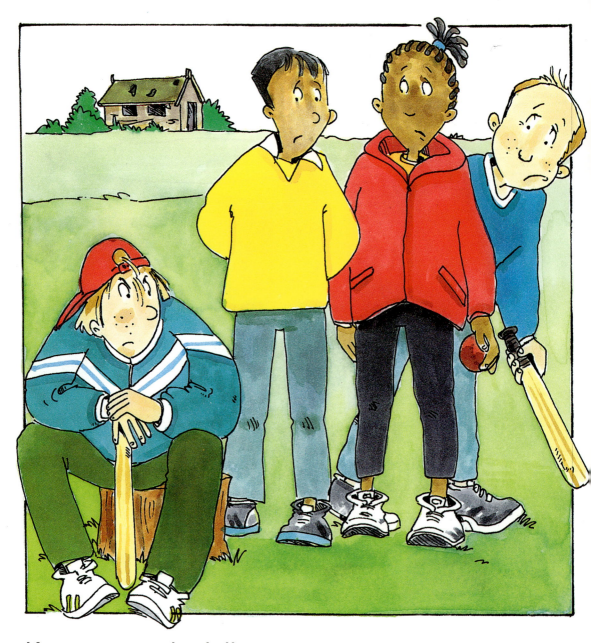

Kev was on the hill.

Ravi hit the ball but Kev got it.

Kev hit the ball into the hut.

"Go and get it, Kev," said Sam.

"No way! No one will go in that hut," said Kev.

"There are bats in that hut," said Kim.

"And there are rats in that hut," said Ravi.

"We will all get the ball. Come on!" said Sam.

Sam, Kim and Ravi went into the hut.

Kev ran up to the hut.

"Is that you, Ravi?" said Kim.

"No, that's not me," said Ravi. "Is that you, Sam?"

"No, that's not me. That's Kev," said Sam.
"Let's get him!"

"Woo-oo! Woo-oo!" said Sam, Kim and Ravi.

Kev ran and ran and ran.